Fact Finders®

HUMANS AND OUR PLANET

HUMANS AND EARTH'S ATMOSPHERE

What's in the air?

Ava Sawyer

raintree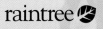

a Capstone company — publishers for children

Raintree is an imprint of Capstone Global Library Limited, a company incorporated in England and Wales having its registered office at 264 Banbury Road, Oxford, OX2 7DY – Registered company number: 6695582

www.raintree.co.uk
myorders@raintree.co.uk

Edited by Nikki Potts
Designed by Philippa Jenkins
Original illustrations © Capstone Global Library Limited 2017
Picture research by Jo Miller
Production by Kathy McColley
Originated by Capstone Global Library Limited
Printed and bound in China

ISBN 978-1-4747-4375-4
21 20 19 18 17
10 9 8 7 6 5 4 3 2 1

British Library Cataloguing in Publication Data
A full catalogue record for this book is available from the British Library.

Acknowledgements
We would like to thank the following for permission to reproduce photographs: Dreamstime: Akulamatiau, 26; Getty Images: Ryan McVay, 25; iStockphoto: LeoPatrizi, 22; NASA: Goddard Space Flight Center/Paul Newman and Marit Jentoft-Nilsen, 19; Newscom: Ambient Images/Peter Bennett, 24, Sipa USA/NASA, 8; Shutterstock: Aerovista Luchtfotografie, 15, airphoto.gr, 10, Crystal-K, 5, designbydx, 11, Ishwar Thakkar, 12, Joseph Sohm, 18, Jurik Peter, 4, littleny, 27, lzf, cover, Matej Kastelic, 23, MOHAMED ABDULRAHEEM, 20–21, Nicku, 9, Rawpixel. com, throughout (background), Rudmer Zwerver, 14, shooarts, 6, testing, 16, 17, Vitoriano Junior, 13

Every effort has been made to contact copyright holders of material reproduced in this book. Any omissions will be rectified in subsequent printings if notice is given to the publisher.

All the internet addresses (URLs) given in this book were valid at the time of going to press. However, due to the dynamic nature of the internet, some addresses may have changed, or sites may have changed or ceased to exist since publication. While the author and publisher regret any inconvenience this may cause readers, no responsibility for any such changes can be accepted by either the author or the publisher.

CONTENTS

WHAT IS THE ATMOSPHERE?

Earth's atmosphere is a blanket of gases that surrounds the planet. From space, our atmosphere looks like a thin blue band of air. The atmosphere has several purposes. It gives plants and animals the carbon dioxide and oxygen they need to survive. The atmosphere protects the planet by acting like a shield, blocking harmful **radiation** and speeding asteroids from outer space. It also helps to control the amount of the sun's energy that reaches Earth's surface. The gases in the atmosphere help to moderate Earth's temperature. They keep it from becoming too hot or too cold for life on Earth.

Sunlight reflects off Earth's atmosphere.

radiation rays of energy given off by certain elements

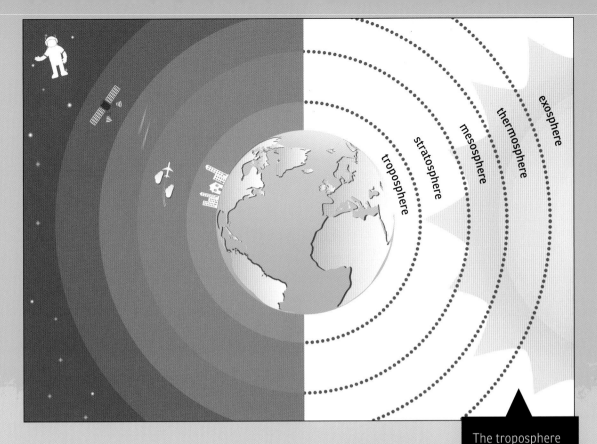

The layers, from innermost to outermost, are labelled: troposphere, stratosphere, mesosphere, thermosphere, exosphere.

The troposphere layer is closest to Earth's surface. The exosphere layer fades into outer space.

Earth's atmosphere is made up of 78 per cent nitrogen, 21 per cent oxygen, 0.93 per cent argon, and 0.038 per cent carbon dioxide. Water vapour is also a part of the atmosphere. It varies between 0 and 4 per cent of the atmosphere. The amount of water vapour depends upon the location on Earth, time of day, time of year and current weather conditions. Earth's atmosphere isn't the same all the way through. The atmosphere is divided into five separate layers. Beginning with the layer closest to the earth and moving outward is the troposphere, stratosphere, mesosphere, thermosphere and exosphere. The layers are made up of different gases and have different **densities**.

density the amount of mass an object or substance has based on a unit of volume

5

TROPOSPHERE

The troposphere is the layer of the atmosphere closest to Earth. It begins at Earth's surface and goes upward between 0 and 11 kilometres (0 and 7 miles). The troposphere is the densest part of the entire atmosphere. It is densest at Earth's surface. The very top of the troposphere is called the tropopause.

The troposphere gets thinner as you move up in the layer. That's why Mount Everest climbers need to bring oxygen tanks with them.

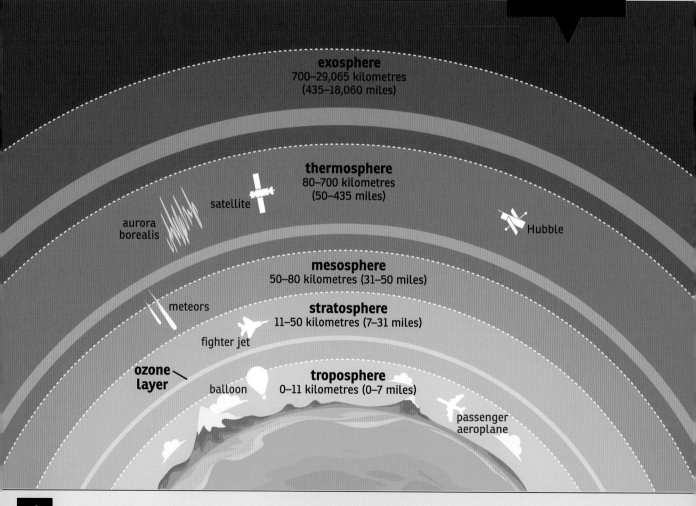

exosphere
700–29,065 kilometres
(435–18,060 miles)

thermosphere
80–700 kilometres
(50–435 miles)

satellite

aurora
borealis

Hubble

mesosphere
50–80 kilometres (31–50 miles)

meteors

stratosphere
11–50 kilometres (7–31 miles)

fighter jet

ozone
layer

balloon

troposphere
0–11 kilometres (0–7 miles)

passenger
aeroplane

STRATOSPHERE

The stratosphere begins just above the tropopause. The highest point of the stratosphere layer stretches 50 kilometres (31 miles) above Earth. In the troposphere, temperature decreases with altitude. The higher you go, the colder it gets.

THE OZONE LAYER

One of the layers in the stratosphere is the **ozone layer**. Ozone is a gas similar to oxygen. Both are made of oxygen atoms. However, oxygen gas has two atoms in its molecule (O_2) and ozone has three (O_3). The ozone layer is a collection of ozone gas found in the upper stratosphere. This layer helps absorb the sun's ultraviolet radiation. When the ozone layer is destroyed, more harmful radiation makes its way to Earth.

Chlorofluorocarbons

One problem of the stratosphere is that any particle that ends up in this layer can stay there for a long time – for months or even years. Ozone-destroying chemicals like chlorofluorocarbons are one concern in the stratosphere. Chlorofluorocarbons (CFCs) are chemicals that contain atoms of carbon, chlorine and fluorine. They are used in the manufacturing of aerosol sprays and can destroy stratospheric ozone.

ozone layer the thin layer of ozone high above Earth's surface that blocks out some of the sun's harmful rays

MESOSPHERE

The mesosphere stretches from about 50 kilometres (31 miles) above Earth to 80 kilometres (50 miles) above Earth. Less is known about the mesosphere than any of the other layers. It's difficult for scientists to study this layer. It's too high for weather balloons and aircraft to fly, and it's too low for satellites.

FACT

To learn more about this layer, scientists from NASA send sounding rockets into the mesosphere. These rockets carry scientific instruments into space. These missions only last between 5 and 20 minutes. During that time scientists are able to obtain new data about this area of the atmosphere.

NASA launches a suborbital sounding rocket carrying student experiments on 26 June 2015.

THERMOSPHERE

This layer of the atmosphere has very hot temperatures. The gases in this layer absorb high-energy radiation, causing extremely high temperatures in the thermosphere. The main parts of air in the upper thermosphere include oxygen atoms, nitrogen atoms and helium.

EXOSPHERE

The highest part of the atmosphere is called the exosphere. There isn't a distinct line between Earth's atmosphere and outer space. The atmosphere eventually gets so thin that it becomes an empty vacuum of space. Some scientists argue that outer space starts much lower in the thermosphere. Others think outer space begins at the edge of the exosphere. They say that atmosphere is still present until the lightest particles, such as hydrogen atoms, start escaping from Earth's gravity and into space. The exosphere is composed almost entirely of hydrogen gas. There are only small amounts of other atmospheric gases like oxygen, helium and carbon dioxide.

The word *exosphere* comes from the Greek words *exo*, which means "outside," and *sphaira*, which means sphere.

THE INDUSTRIAL REVOLUTION

In the modern era, humans have made a big impact on the atmosphere. Humans began burning **fossil fuels** during the Industrial Revolution in the 1800s. A fossil fuel is made up of **organic** materials formed from plants and animals that died millions of years ago. Newly invented machines during this time needed energy to run. This energy came from the burning of the fossil fuel coal. Soon, coal smoke filled the sky. Some cities were so polluted it looked like night-time in the middle of the day.

A fossil fuel power plant releases smoke into the air while operating.

fossil fuel natural fuel formed from the remains of plants and animals; coal, oil and natural gas are fossil fuels

organic items that are obtained from something once living and that contain the element carbon

Air pollution fills the air in Beijing, China, in 2015.

These types of conditions remained in some cities into the mid-1900s. They are still present in places that lack air pollution regulations. The city of Beijing, China, for example, is highly polluted. The majority of homes and power plants still burn coal. When conditions are really severe in Beijing, people have to wear masks. They also have to limit outdoor activities as much as possible.

In the beginning of the Industrial Revolution, some factory owners thought it didn't matter how much smoke they put into the air. Over time, though, humans have learned how dangerous it is to treat the atmosphere this way.

CHAPTER 3

FOSSIL FUELS

Fossil fuels formed from dead plants and animals. Their bodies were buried in the earth. Other layers piled on top. Great pressure caused the organic materials to turn to rock. Some of this organic material became coal. Living things are made up of carbon, so fossil fuels also have carbon. When fossil fuels are burned, carbon turns into carbon dioxide. Then it is released into the atmosphere.

Coal is combustible, meaning it burns easily.

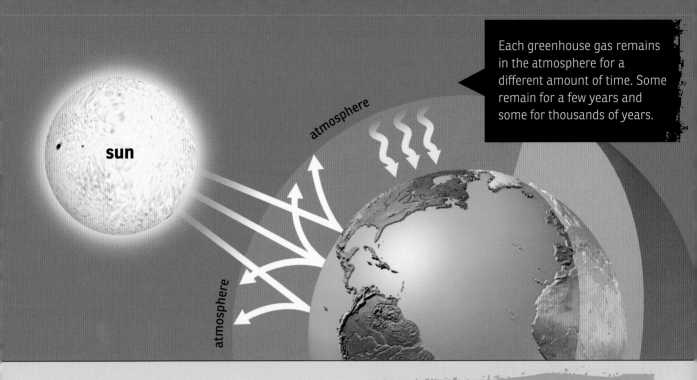

sun

atmosphere

atmosphere

Each greenhouse gas remains in the atmosphere for a different amount of time. Some remain for a few years and some for thousands of years.

Carbon dioxide is a **greenhouse gas**. This means it traps heat in Earth's atmosphere. Carbon dioxide is the most important gas for controlling Earth's temperature. A large increase in carbon dioxide causes a rise in Earth's temperature. The increased heating of Earth is called **global warming**. Many scientists think global warming is partly caused by an increase in carbon dioxide in the atmosphere from burning fossil fuels.

Greenhouse gases

Some greenhouse gases are naturally part of the atmosphere and act like a blanket for Earth. Sunlight travels through the atmosphere and warms Earth. When the heat rises back up from Earth and re-enters the atmosphere, the greenhouse gases trap the heat and help keep Earth warm. Without greenhouse gases Earth would be a very cold place. There are both naturally occurring greenhouse gases and synthetic, or human-made, greenhouse gases.

greenhouse gas gas in a planet's atmosphere that traps heat energy from the sun

global warming the idea that Earth's temperature is slowly rising

Carbon dioxide levels remained fairly constant until modern times. Then there was a large spike in carbon dioxide levels. Ever since the Industrial Revolution, the amount of carbon dioxide in the atmosphere has risen.

Fossil fuels are burned in many ways for many reasons. People use coal and natural gas to heat their houses. Power plants burn coal and natural gas to make electricity. Factories use these energy sources to power their machines and equipment. In addition, humans use fossil fuels for many types of transportation.

FACT

Scientists study ice cores from Antarctica to determine what atmospheric carbon dioxide levels were before the Industrial Revolution.

Coal is burned at a power plant to produce electricity.

A wind turbine farm in Volerak in the Netherlands is a clean energy source.

Environmental scientists have done tests to see which fossil fuel releases the most carbon dioxide. Their studies show that it is coal. It puts two times more carbon dioxide into the atmosphere than natural gas. Carbon dioxide isn't the only gas released when coal is burned. Nitrogen oxides, sulphur dioxide and dangerous heavy metals such as mercury are released too.

People are trying to use more "clean energy" sources. A clean energy source is one that doesn't burn fossil fuels. Some examples are wind energy, solar energy and water energy. Solar and wind farms are built in many places around the world. Dams use water to provide hydroelectric power. Areas with volcanic activity can use geothermal power. All of these options provide energy that does not negatively impact the atmosphere.

Fossil fuels are used to power many types of transportation. Cars, trains, ships and jets all use fossil fuels. Scientists have measured the amount of carbon dioxide released from each type of transportation. They have found that road transportation gives off the most carbon dioxide.

FACT

Carbon dioxide isn't the only type of gas that vehicles release into the atmosphere. Carbon monoxide, an extremely poisonous gas, is also released. Sulphur dioxide, nitrogen dioxide, benzene and formaldehyde also come from cars.

A man in Beijing, China, wears a mask due to high smog conditions.

All of the gases released from vehicles into the atmosphere form **smog**. It is thick like fog and is very dirty. Smog has been linked to many health problems. People have a hard time breathing it in. Their hearts can also be harmed. People with asthma, chronic bronchitis and cardiovascular disease are at particular risk in smoggy conditions.

smog fog that has become mixed with smoke or other pollution and hangs in the air over a city or industrial area

17

AEROSOLS AND PLASTICS

Manufactured products also harm the atmosphere. **Aerosols** and plastics are particularly dangerous.

Aerosol spray is a substance that is enclosed in a can under pressure. It is released in a fine mist. Hairspray, whipped cream, deodorants, air fresheners, cleaners and spray paint are all examples of aerosol sprays. The liquid isn't the only thing that is released from the can when it is sprayed. Gases are also released at the same time.

Aerosol sprays were invented in the 1920s in the United States. For many decades manufacturers used chlorofluorocarbon (CFC) gases in aerosol sprays. In the 1970s scientists discovered that these gases were causing major problems for Earth's atmosphere. The ozone layer of the atmosphere was being destroyed by the CFCs. Scientists believed that a giant hole in the ozone over Antarctica was caused by chlorofluorocarbons.

Local recycling facilities should be contacted for information on how to properly dispose of aerosols in your area.

aerosol a mass of tiny particles mixed with air or another gas

Since 1979, scientists have recorded the changing size of the ozone hole (shown in blue) over Antarctica.

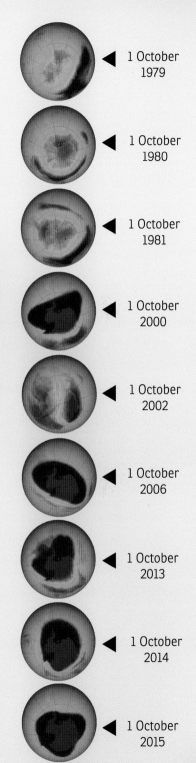

1 October 1979

1 October 1980

1 October 1981

1 October 2000

1 October 2002

1 October 2006

1 October 2013

1 October 2014

1 October 2015

Twenty-eight countries from around the world met in 1987. They promised to pass laws that prevented companies from using CFCs in their products. Since then these dangerous gases have been removed from all kinds of products. Aerosol sprays, refrigerators, air-conditioning systems and fire extinguishers no longer use them.

Even though aerosol sprays in today's market don't contain CFCs, they still contain **hydrocarbons**. These are believed to increase global warming as well.

FACT

Ozone levels have made a comeback. But scientists believe it will still take a long time for all CFCs to be completely removed from the atmosphere. These gases have a long atmospheric life span. The ones already in the atmosphere will likely remain there for over 100 years. Scientists hope that by 2070, the ozone layer will be back to normal levels.

hydrocarbon chemical compound made up mainly of hydrogen and carbon atoms

PLASTICS

The main ingredient used to make plastics comes from petrochemicals, an oil-based material. Around 8 per cent of the world's oil production is used to make plastics. Oil is a fossil fuel, and burning it increases carbon dioxide. Plastic production increases every year by about 9 per cent.

The manufacturing of plastics impacts the atmosphere in negative ways. So does the destruction of plastics. Plastics make up approximately 10 per cent of the world's **landfills**. Plastics do not quickly break down on their own. Some experts believe it will take hundreds or thousands of years for them to break down. That's why they are often burned. Yet when plastics are burned, they release huge amounts of carbon gases into the atmosphere.

Plastic waste fills a disposal site in Thilafushi, an island in the Maldives.

landfill a place where rubbish is buried

HOW CAN HUMANS HELP?

There are many ways that humans can help the atmosphere. If every person on the planet did something small, the results on a global scale could be quite astounding.

Riding bikes instead of driving has a positive impact on the environment.

TRANSPORTATION

One thing that people can do is try to limit transportation that burns fossil fuels. Instead of driving alone, people can take public transport or share cars. They can also use other kinds of vehicles, such as bicycles, or walk when possible. With fewer cars on the roads, there will be fewer vehicle emissions released into the atmosphere.

If driving a vehicle is necessary, be sure the tires are properly inflated. When a car has low air pressure in its tires, the car will use more fuel. Also try to use the air conditioning sparingly, as this also uses more fuel. Don't let your car sit and idle with the engine running. This puts a lot of vehicle emissions into the atmosphere without the car moving anywhere.

Alternative solutions

Some car manufacturers are trying to help the atmosphere. They are developing new types of vehicles that burn less fuel and give off fewer pollutants. Some even burn clean fuels such as biofuels, which are made from plants. Electric cars are usually a "clean" transport option. However, they aren't 100 per cent friendly to the environment. They run on batteries, which have to be powered. The batteries get their power by plugging into a power source. This power source may be fuelled by fossil fuels.

An energy-efficient car recharges by plugging into a power source.

PLANT TREES

Another way that people can help the atmosphere is to plant more trees. Trees take carbon dioxide out of the atmosphere and release oxygen into it. This is why the rainforest is often called Earth's "lungs". The more trees we have on the planet, the better it is for the atmosphere. Also consider growing other plants such as indoor houseplants and garden plants. Any plant will help lower carbon dioxide and increase oxygen in the atmosphere.

Trees and other plants give off oxygen and help filter the air.

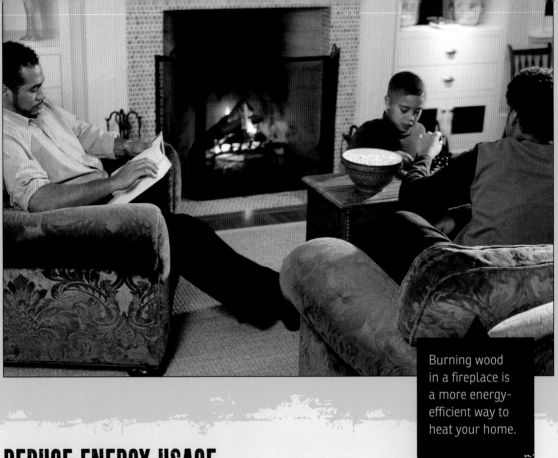

Burning wood in a fireplace is a more energy-efficient way to heat your home.

REDUCE ENERGY USAGE

Many electric power plants burn some kind of fossil fuel to make energy. The more electricity used, the more fossil fuels need to be burned to make electricity. People should try to limit the amount of heating and cooling they use in their homes, offices and buildings as much as possible. In winter, wear sweaters and use lots of blankets instead of turning up the heating. Keep blinds closed at night to stop the heat from flowing out of the windowpane. In summer, open windows at night to cool down the house. You can keep blinds closed during the day to limit how much sunlight warms up the house.

BE SELECTIVE

Don't use things you will throw away after only one use, such as plastic water bottles. They fill up landfills unnecessarily. Use a water bottle you can wash and use over and over again. Plastic shopping bags are another example of something that can harm Earth. Bring your own cloth, reusable bags to the shops instead.

Remember that every little bit helps. You may not think that your efforts are making a difference, but they are. You can also make a difference by encouraging others to care about the atmosphere and do their part too. The more people who get involved in this effort, the better the planet will be for everyone.

Reusable shopping bags are a positive alternative to using plastic bags.

1200s

Late 13th century: King Edward I of England bans the burning of sea-coal in London because it causes air pollution; the ban is unsuccessful.

Late 18th century & early 19th century: The Industrial Revolution brings about large-scale use of coal and intensified air and water pollution.

1700s

1852

Robert Smith, the government's Alkali inspector, invents the phrase "acid rain". He is the first to show the relationship between acid rain and atmospheric pollution.

Chemist Arie Haagen-Smit discovers nitrogen oxides mixed with sunlight form ozone – a main component of smog.

1948

1952

The Great London Smog. At least 4,000 people die over the course of several days after pollutants from factories and fireplaces mix with air condensation.

The Clean Air Act is established to focus on reducing smoke pollution.

1956

1961

The United Kingdom establishes the first coordinated national air pollution monitoring network, the National Survey.

The catalytic converter, a device used to significantly cut auto emissions and reduce air pollution, is invented.

1975

1980s

The Montreal Protocol is established. This international treaty helps protect the ozone layer by phasing out substances responsible for harming the ozone.

The Environmental Protection Act is established. A system of pollution control for the most potentially polluting industrial processes is put in place.

1990

1994

United Nations General Assembly announces 16 September as International Ozone Day.

GLOSSARY

aerosol a mass of tiny particles mixed with air or another gas

density the amount of mass an object or substance has based on a unit of volume

fossil fuel natural fuel formed from the remains of plants and animals; coal, oil and natural gas are fossil fuels

global warming the idea that Earth's temperature is slowly rising

greenhouse gas gas in a planet's atmosphere that traps heat energy from the sun

hydrocarbon chemical compound made up mainly of hydrogen and carbon atoms

landfill a place where rubbish is buried

organic items that are obtained from something once living and that contain the element carbon

ozone layer the thin layer of ozone high above Earth's surface that blocks out some of the sun's harmful rays

radiation rays of energy given off by certain elements

smog fog that has become mixed with smoke or other pollution and hangs in the air over a city or industrial area

FIND OUT MORE

Are Humans Damaging the Atmosphere? (Earth Debates),
  Catherine Chambers (Raintree, 2016)

Reduce, Reuse, Recycle, Rebecca Rissman (Wayland, 2017)

Renewable Energy, Nancy Dickmann (Wayland, 2017)

WEBSITES

www.bbc.co.uk/education/clips/zbdyr82
Visit this BBC website to find out about carbon dioxide in
the atmosphere.

climatekids.nasa.gov/greenhouse-cards/
This NASA website has information about greenhouse
gases – what they are and what they do.

**www.dkfindout.com/uk/earth/structure-earth/earths-
atmosphere**
This interactive website has information about Earth's
atmosphere and its different layers.

COMPREHENSION QUESTIONS

- Name and give one detail about each of Earth's atmospheric layers.

- Harmful gases released from vehicles produce smog. What is smog?

- How does using reusable water bottles help the atmosphere?

INDEX